Waking Up Alice

When Procrastination Wastes Precious Time

A collection of poetry

Letitia D. Fowler

BALBOA.
PRESS
A DIVISION OF HAY HOUSE

Balboa Press books may be ordered through booksellers or by contacting:

Balboa Press
A Division of Hay House
1663 Liberty Drive
Bloomington, IN 47403
www.balboapress.com
1 (877) 407-4847

Because of the dynamic nature of the Internet, any web addresses or links contained in this book may have changed since publication and may no longer be valid. The views expressed in this work are solely those of the author and do not necessarily reflect the views of the publisher, and the publisher hereby disclaims any responsibility for them.

The author of this book does not dispense medical advice or prescribe the use of any technique as a form of treatment for physical, emotional, or medical problems without the advice of a physician, either directly or indirectly. The intent of the author is only to offer information of a general nature to help you in your quest for emotional and spiritual well-being. In the event you use any of the information in this book for yourself, which is your constitutional right, the author and the publisher assume no responsibility for your actions.

Any people depicted in stock imagery provided by Thinkstock are models, and such images are being used for illustrative purposes only. Certain stock imagery © Thinkstock.

Printed in the United States of America.

ISBN: 978-1-4525-1833-6 (sc)
ISBN: 978-1-4525-1835-0 (hc)
ISBN: 978-1-4525-1834-3 (e)
Library of Congress Control Number: 2014912462

Balboa Press rev. date: 08/06/2014

This book is dedicated to GOD
My Lord and Savior Jesus Christ
Thank you Holy Spirit for your constant reminder
That I am creative and poetic
Gingerly, I submit my first seed offering

Honor the Lord with thy substance,
and with the first fruits of all thine increase:
So shall thy barns be filled with plenty
and thy presses shall burst out with new wine.
Proverbs 3:9-10

Acknowledgments

I thank my mother, *Patricia Josephine Fowler*. Who held my hand one day and apologized for not remembering my childhood. I cherish everyday I get a glimpse of her old self. These past six years care giving for her have been a blessing in disguise. Time well spent in reflection and prayer allowing my gift and calling to be realized.

To my husband, **Dennis Downs**, thank you for taking over care of my mother when I became disabled with Congestive Heart Failure. Your help & support are greatly appreciated.

To **Bishop Noel Jones**, thank you for all your deeply inspirational & thought provoking sermons preached and bible classes taught. Every time you told the congregation to "get up and shake yourselves" I felt it in my soul. Thank you, thank you, thank you.

Finally, to the Balboa Press publishing team, thank you for answering every phone call and responding to every email. With your professional help, I was able to get "my words from the page to the people."-Balboa Press Publishing

In loving memory

My cousin Lois
My college roommate Maria from Detroit

Contents

Introduction

Now is the time

I thought I'd have to lose weight to write
like really
what could I have to say
that would be relevant anyway
But time kept on passing
and reality often illusive
became a strong task master

I thought I could hide
and not live life
just wait to die
But God
was relentless
in His pursuit of my happiness
and His reality has no respect of persons
Spiritually within
my dreams were still alive

Quietly I existed
anonymously roaming
in isolation
The strength of my silence
magnified the powerful force of my intentions

Inside is a gift that must see the light of day
yet every morning I rise
opening up my big brown eyes
breathing

still thinking wondering if I've left living too late
So I prayed
keeping a tight grip on sanity
just barely
I see me trying
can't figure out why I'm still alive
when others seemingly more gifted have died
even at 50 I rationalized
obedience is better than sacrifice
So I write
armed with a community college degree
over 20 years old now means nothing seemingly
SAT scores 469 the scale screaming 432
I've got 400's all over the place
and still I can hear **God** say
Do it anyway
Do it for Me
Take the opportunity
given only to the living
and tell those still waiting
It's Now time for waking
Now is the time to be a blessing
Now is the time to honor God and give Him the Glory
live your dream now
Right Now
Now is the time

"If there's a book you want to read,
but it hasn't been written yet,
then you must write it."
-Toni Morrison

Until Now

I thought to wait Until
Until I felt smart enough
Until I was small enough
Until I felt saved enough
Until I thought I was cute enough
But I'll never be that smart
And I didn't even know what saved enough was
And losing weight well that's my life long battle anyhow
So I might as well go on ahead and get the job done
Cause there's no way I'm dying and leaving this earth with
all these words screaming to get out unsaid
The material presented may not be littered with literary
content
and may seem too redundant for the academically astute
But it's my truth
And its only relevance or significance is the fact
I wrote it
The whole point of having a voice is owning it and using it
So with both hands I took the chance
I give to you my first seed offering
All poems and prose following
Sing and scream
My life
My world
My dreams
Until Now
In my voice
From my mind
Through my eyes
Inspired by the Holy Spirit

These pages are filled with my experiences
Like a baby on trembling feet
I take the first small step
And present this gift

Waking Up Alice
"in silence these words could not be kept"

Sitting in the Pews

In service sitting in the pews
all dressed up fine in my Jimmy Choo's
I thought I was listening
Bishop Jones is always saying
"looking like *Alice* in Wonderland"
what was I missing
when the preached word
only found my stony ground Matt13:5
here one day and gone the next
Getting caught up in emotions
and forgot the text
that was the mess
I found myself in
Why get offended
And blame it on who
When studying and meditating on God's words
Was what I was suppose to do

I learned that hard lesson right
as my conscious mind evolved
hearing the word on Wednesday and Sunday nights
It took listening and hearing
over and over again
for the word to finally sink in
and then putting it to practice
was where my real journey begins

So the next time I'm in service
Sitting in the Pews
in my Jimmy Choo's

I'll be spending my worship time listening for clues
of how I can use the word to get me through
obstacles, trials and sickness too

The good word preached
is now falling on my good ground
can you hear the quiet sound
of a conscious soul listening

Still is the night when the Spirit whispers
when God chooses you for His purpose
destiny is your course
it takes you first
to the problem
to the pain
and fills you with the solution
Your minuet piece of it anyhow
No matter how intricate
It has an intrinsic value
That solves and answers

So when you see what no one else sees
Know its yours
"so go get your blessing" –Mary Mary
And know that sitting in those pews
a gift is hidden
and it's you
So wake up 𝒜𝓁𝒾𝒸𝑒
And be about your Father's business

"Sometimes I feel discouraged
and think my works are in vain
but then the Holy Spirit revives my soul again…"
-Walter Hawkins
I Won't Be Satisfied

An unlocked door

There was an unlocked door that no one saw
It seemed only natural for me to go in
I was unprepared and ill-equipped
To deal with what I was about to witness
Yet somehow I knew early experience
Was key to this development

There was an unlocked door that no one saw
It seemed only natural for me to go in
I was arrested by the unknown
frozen to the spot
overwhelmed by the occasion
I couldn't breathe

Whatever you imagine destiny to be
Reality is everything
The struggles the hardships the waiting all that waiting
I walked in to my purpose that day
The day I saw the unlocked door
All those little steps and slow unveiling
Left me unprepared and ill equipped
To deal with
What has been a tedious life rehearsal
Getting me ready to live my life out loud
In bold relief
And all those gone before me didn't get to see
What God has apparently tailored made for me

An unlocked door
With the Holy Spirit whispering

This is your dream you're entering
Then I knew it
What was meant to be
Came to me as decreed
Walking simply
I was free from my naiveté
Following where God leads
Showed me things
Supernatural things
Plainly hidden from the prudent
Told me don't be disobedient
Just walk right on through it

There was an unlocked door that no one saw
The Holy Spirit leads me
Straight to my purpose and destiny
Can you see yours
Don't be afraid to take it
It's right there through those unlocked doors

a living suicide

the hardest thing I ever had to do
was to learn how to be alive
I stand with a defined perspective
my concentrated experiences
not necessarily different
caused me to understand my divinely specific role in life
despite my continuous denial of my condition
I had to learn to walk worthy of my position
existing for the most part as invisible
I was ignored
and deemed unqualified
I ain't going to lie
most of the time I didn't even try
my hidden torment seems fake now that I'm awake
it was like
a living suicide
intentionally and on purpose
we pull to the table to kill ourselves
"Why sit we here till we die?" IIKings7:3
is there any life
faith
fight
hope
dream left in you
continuously ignoring instructions
like we've lost all direction
self medicating
with remedies the world chase after
until we're like in a living coma
consciously unconscious

intentionally and on purpose
we pretend over and over again
as if by osmosis
something mystical magical will change us
with more lies
the hardest thing I ever had to do was learn how to be alive

I stand
with a defined perspective
my concentrated experiences were not necessarily different
from yours
just divinely specific to me
trying not to feel that pain
or deal with those disturbing emotions
was useless
we hide openly pretending
going through the motions
stuffing and numbing
ignoring and dummying down our intellect
refusing to exist on a conscious plain
avoiding the obvious pain
sabotaging
interfering and damaging
what should be a sanctified life
we engage in certain activities
that ultimately are destructive
not because we don't know it's killing us
but because we feel powerless to stop it (on our own)
addictive behaviors are dangerous
It's like we're slowly dying
a living suicide

The hardest thing I ever had to do
was to learn how to be alive
I stand with a defined perspective
my experiences not necessarily different
just divinely specific
conquering the beast whatever your affliction
has to be dealt with on a conscious level
boldly and unapologetically
we have to set out to erase all our insecurities and all our
doubts
and learn to believe what God said before
before the first lie was told
before we ever realized who we were and what our purpose
was
before we got sidetracked deceived tricked by the enemy
any associations to early childhood traumas
presents a distorted reality
now it's time to fix it
now it's time to get it together
handle your business man up to the challenge of life
instead of disappearing behind fake walls of pretense
escaping in weed food sex and alcohol
that won't solve the problems we're all experiencing
my identity was wrapped up in how I think about myself
and it made me rebellious
pride kept alive something that should of died
but we keep pain alive by burying it under addictions
we bury alive something that should not have permission to
abort our mission
unresolved issues that haunt and linger
are demonic intentions targeted
with a pointed trigger finger at our soul

we should be so bold
as to take back control
of our life of this fight
when did we stop trying to free ourselves
instead we walk like the defeated
a living suicide
let the truth come alive
see it for what it is and know you're not alone
and that wall in your mind that tried
to separate your for your destiny
falls down flat
bricks start flying and heavy chains dropping off to nothing
and see possibilities loom limitless
but it's up to us
to realize until it is finished nothing can stop us
God gave us a special way of dealing with problems
when God filled you He gave you everything
you'd ever need to succeed
break the silence
speak to your situation
and demand it get under your feet
stop disconnecting from your intellect
pretending you don't know the solution
or haven't heard the answers
listen
push past the pain
stop being careless with the conscious mind
losing yourself inside the addiction
addictions that control us
keeping us anesthetized drunk and too weak
we're asleep
walking ineffectively

but it's time to wake up
and get our mission back on track
we have to learn new behaviors new mind sets
new attitudes new determinations
renewing and transforming our minds in Christ
is our objective and it starts now
don't live
a living suicide
live
a holy living God kind of life

My steps were measured

Each foot print rehearsed
Without memory of knowing
Still I found myself
Exactly where I was supposed to be

Revealed time shows itself
To the hearts and minds of the believers

You can not conceive what has not already been
Episodic series of combined lives
Exist in our memories often forgotten
It's with each gift expressed
We evolve to everlasting
We leave nothing left but an empty vessel
Our chosen destinies exposed
And shows each dreamer their choice
When chosen we find our voice
We walk in the light
that is our collective experiences
Those obedient to the call
Are lead by a deeper glory
Often their untold story

God whispers
Angels stand at attention
And heaven releases provisional blessings

The synchronization of time
Often feels invented or contrived
As if thought could change a preordained life

Words spoken however
Have their own inherent power
An overflowing heart must speak
So let goodness be the thing you must think of
And watch life unfold in the miraculous

With each measured step
I knew nothing
Until it was revealed to me
And still without seeing I kept moving only believing
Everything would be as it's suppose to be

Assigned and selected
We are given to benevolence
Measured to capacity
We are judged by our living in our giving
So leave nothing left but empty
And find fulfillment eternal

In each unique expression
We evolve
Immortal souls perfected

From the moment I entered the earth
My steps were measured
Seeking direction
I moved forward
Led by the light
Trusting the voice of God
My Lord and Savior Jesus Christ
My steps were measured
Each foot print rehearsed
Each foot print rehearsed

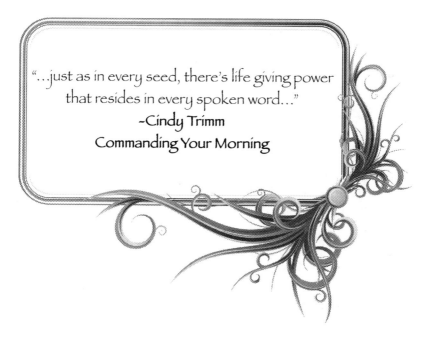

"...just as in every seed, there's life giving power that resides in every spoken word..."
-Cindy Trimm
Commanding Your Morning

Talitha Cumi - Mark 5:41

When Jesus gives a command
Even the dead rise saying Lord here I am
Taking my hand He told me
Letitia, come to me
Wake up and see yourself free
I'm right here with you
Always

Rising from my sick bed I took the necessary step
Putting one foot in front of the other
And before I knew it
I was walking out on faith
Believing
My conflict had been in the doing
Not in the knowing
The simplicity threw me
I couldn't see the outcome
How was this going to be that
The how was not my concern
When God says get up
Talitha Cumi to me translates
Letitia come on

I can do all things
Christ gives me the strength
Learning everyday to be content
Is another conflict
All I want to hear Jesus say
Is well done
Forgiven my sins no longer exist

Looking up to the Son
Adjusting my concept of success
I have found
I'm succeeding just by being born
I erase from my mind every mistake that tried to take away
my peace
I will not let satan defeat me or cheat me of my destiny
I've set my face to God resting in expectancy
Anticipating hope the catalyst that moves my mountains
Knowing nothing can block or stop my purpose
We wait for the final curtain
Giving our Lord a standing ovation
He set His image in our hearts
Divine assignments was His to impart
It all started when He reached for my hand
And said
Talitha Cumi
Damsel please stand
Lord here I am
With tears in my eyes
I moved forward and watched
The red sea part
Water flowing from a rock
Ravens with bread in their mouth
Manna falling from heaven
Being forgiven over again like seventy times seven
How the widows mite was a true sacrifice
Paying tithes and free will offerings was doing my money
right
Saving more than I spent finally made sense
Being blessed to be blessing
Made my life more relevant

The evidence of The Cross makes God's love extraordinarily significant
More important than dying being an inconvenience
Christ's obedience is way beyond comprehension or comparison
I can't stress how powerful I felt
Knowing my foundation was built on that love
It's Jesus name I trust
And with every praise that's left my mouth
I walk this earth convinced
No matter the situations or consequence
My gift is commissioned from God and heaven sent
Talitha Cumi
Is my defense

O Daniel

We ask ourselves
if we can believe God through it all
then the devil hears our whispered cries
and tries to make us fall
some of us have scrapped knees from being thrown to the
ground
others have silent screams that make no sound at all
like King Darius yelling through the rock
covering the lion's den
we all want to know
are you still holding on
O Daniel is your God able to save you once again

my relationship with my heavenly Father
dictates that I acknowledge this one truth
whether perpetuated allowed or divinely assigned
I have to keep my mind on Christ
and know I'm not alone in this fight
with angels encamped around as a hedge of protection
we rise everyday from every situation
knowing that our God is truly able
to deliver us from all our troubles
but if not
we still won't bow

having lost everything more than once
and ending up broke
I will not choke on the bitter pill called pride of life
but rather I drive away lingering doubt
sent to deceive me like Eve

with nothing but this gift left in me
I can always start again from the beginning
knowing the Holy Spirit knows just where to put me
and the last shall be first
Even with all my hesitancy procrastination reigning supreme
from ridiculous to impossible
I can believe God through it all
He may not stop me from being thrown in the fire
but He'll give me strength enough to survive it
and if at the end of each day I can still say
O Daniel is your God able
O King live forever
my God is truly able
Then I know victory is coming my way

I was set apart
Isolated for an appointed time
going through a process
gradually developing
in my temporary environment
Secluded
I was blocked from intrusion
and grew strong
knowing
He has equipped me
for showing
something unique to me
I can breathe
Free
in this controlled and cultivated atmosphere
like a baby in a incubator
I became aware
endued from on high
that I was under development
even before I was born
before I even entered the world
God told me
Promises
in my capsulated setting
assured me with trusting
filled me with loving
Blessed me with an anointing

Everything that I ever wanted
and needed to succeed
was designed with my creative ability
in my mother's womb

Gifted
He released me
I grew from a inseminated egg
to an embryo
and in a little while
a girl child was born to the world
Gravity holds me down
on the surface as earthbound
for now
in this solitary confinement
I existed
learning knowing growing and becoming
forever changing
accepting Jesus as Lord and Savior
was a no brainier
filled to overflowing with the Holy Spirit
The Truth slayer
I lift my hands and praise my God
for bringing me into this world
Nurtured He kept me alive
for such a time as this
No matter how invisible
My life has been until this
I present my gift still under development
To the process of learning
I commit
I was isolated for an appointed time
Until I knew what all God's promises really meant
The key to releasing them is using my gift
I write
to prove
They do exist

this is my life

every time i forget
my mind gets pushed back into oblivion
this total sense of nothingness
screws with my equilibrium
how can i exist without blatant consciousness
one minute thinking and then i'm dreaming
always forgetting
what should be done
where i should be
it's crazy
i fight with myself
it's like some strange satanic spell
procrastination has become an assassination of my gifts and
time
speaking out loud
i will not allow it to persist to detain my gift from its purpose
this is my life
and i get one chance to get it right
i reach into oblivion and beyond and snatch my gift
from the devils hand
i make my stand
i dig up my talents left buried in unconsciousness
i shake loose the chains on my brain that had me dreaming
far too long
knowing as a man thinks in his heart so is he Proverbs 23:7
so i scream my release
i scream i am free
i scream into the blackness where fear lives and
procrastination sits
turning on the light

i awake the promise buried deep inside
i make my stand keeping that hope alive
this is my life
God saved me for a purpose
and figuring it out is what life is about
and we dictate its outcome
God and me
together we agree together we decide
my destiny
God's divine incentive and my free will thinking align
harmonized and synchronized
i reign in my idle willed mind
and chime
this is my life
and i will not allow the devil to turn it upside down inside
out like some three ringed circus
i was born for a reason
God gave it to me
i am the me God created
and everything He ever promised is still there waiting for me
and i'm taking what's mine
ain't no time for crying
so just wipe those tears from your eyes
and holler
this is my life
this *is* my one life to live

Evicted

It was blown all out of proportion
What a ridiculous accusation
Was Eve's pontification
Getting kicked out of Eden
Cursed all generations
Staring in the river lost
Look what our disobedience cost
We stood in the garden
With no clothes on
Stunned
Spinning in circles wondering what to do
You can't tell God
I won't go
When God says get out
Even tithes and offerings
Can't get you by
So don't even try
Might as well keep your money in your pockets
Angels and a flaming sword
Locked it

He told you clearly and succinctly
So what were you thinking?
There's a reason we've got two ears and one mouth
Listen and pay attention
And maybe the next lesson will hold your conviction

Evicted
When a little lie covers the whole truth

When Life Gets Mean

When life gets mean
and distorts everything
I feel sorry for Eve
who had to remember everything specifically
God and Adam said don't eat
but she added to the serpent
we can't even touch it
that's not what the man said
and a door opened with a crack
snake skin boots and all
and he walks right on in
twisting words designed to confuse
but rules is rules
if you've lived long enough
you know
some things you just can't touch or eat
God ain't playing

When life gets mean
and distorts every living thing
I remember Lot's wife
when she told him to curse God and die
you know she lost her mind
when all her kids up and died

try as I might
I can't stretch my brain to believe
double or nothing was actually what that means
can somebody say
that's too much

yet when life gets mean
and distorts everything
I'm still thinking
even with a barren womb
and no place to call home
I know I'm right where I belong
I won't complain

when things get funky
and nothing
makes sense
I'm taking solace
in knowing
I'm not Eve
at least all of humanity isn't teetering on the brink
of what I think or believe
or could it be
individually and collectively He put us in charge of the whole
thing
and its with that semblance of responsibility
that I've got to express my gift to the best of my ability

no I didn't go to Yale
and I don't have "long luxurious blond hair"
thanks Whoopi
or a million dollars to spare
but who cares
so when life gets mean
and distorts every living thing
start reading your Bible
it'll put everything in right perspective
we ain't the only ones suffering

the challenges of life becomes a trophy
of life eternal
we all have a reason to live
even when life gets mean
then mean gets the gift
that lifts us to our everlasting

Forgive Us

Slithering to the earth he saw woman and thought
Ahh.. the weaker vessel or so it seems
easier to deceive easier to please easier to be
and angels mated with men (women)
and giants were in the land
apparently they have no female angels in heaven
the devil perverts and convinces to convert
and homosexuality gave birth
All because he was jealous of Eve
his distorted views destroys every living being
deceit and confusion reigns supreme
kicked out of heaven
Chaucer says better to rule in hell
It's foolishness personified
we've stopped thinking listening to the devil
like sheep we're led to the slaughter
don't follow that copycat father of lies
God is grieved
Father Forgive Us please
His long suffering Love tells much
if we'd just listen and learn to believe
we'd be more like Daniel
with courage consistently
then evil can't be free

Yet from the beginning of time
Women have adopted that strange audacity
first Eve
walks up to her man with eyes all knowing
long hair flowing

and he did eat
ain't nobody saying nothing
they just stopped thinking
and two words were introduced
Forgive Us
how many times
did Delilah lay her head in Sampson's lap
wait a minute in my Bible they flipped that
Hmmm…. could be why he was so weak I'm just saying

Between Bathsheba's baths and Salome's dance
Men then didn't stand a chance

And we let the devil use us
Father please Forgive Us

the devil keeps using those same old moves
becoming bolder the longer we let abomination reside
we sink deeper still
releasing our will
can't you feel the total disconnect
it's our heavenly Father we reject
our hearts we must protect
Forgive Us
It's not too late to repent
that's why Jesus was sent
and satan is filled with contempt
what is man that God is mindful of him
His beloved creation for one
jealousy breeds from the pit
God sent Jesus to die for us to redeem us having already
forgiven us

all we have to do is believe it and accept the gift of salvation
shake loose the chains on your brain
and win this war on your knees can the church say amen
as a modern day woman I know without Christ
I can do nothing right anyway
God completes me
without Him in my life
I know with a surety something essential is missing
Father
Forgive Us
Please
We bob and weave between
Knowing the power of God's love
To shrugging off destiny for pleasures temporary
God is grieved
By how short sighted our vision
When eternity is filled with joy everlasting
To the woman first
There's more to you then what's under your skirt
And if men protected and honored us
despite our sultry inclinations
Then nobody would get hurt
And we wouldn't have to be yelling
Father please
Forgive Us

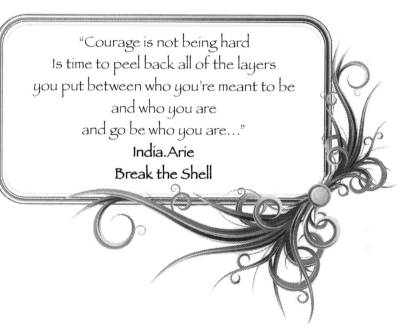

"Courage is not being hard
Is time to peel back all of the layers
you put between who you're meant to be
and who you are
and go be who you are..."
India.Arie
Break the Shell

great pretender

clamoring thoughts and fraudulent dispositions
fought for equal time to confuse tender young minds
mystical soothsayers with phony open eyed prayers
trying to vanquish lies and cognitive resistance
magicians casting spells
with shadows and smoking mirrors
there's an impostor among us
the father of lies
infiltrating and perpetuating
sin to the lost
like zombies mindless and robotic we follow
the chaotic flames of fire we've swallowed
lies told so long now right seems wrong
and on and on it goes
sin has kicked the hinges off the closet
boldly and egotistical an ambush has been parlayed
postulating and hypnotizing with fake disguises
now who's really hiding
the Christians are missing
can't you see there's a charlatan in the midst
it's razzamatazz time
when the rapture begins
three years of wedded bliss but hell is on God's list
satan's squint-y eyed looks they've missed
a Cheshire cat grin fades quick
twisted words used to trick
even lessons in Sunday school classes don't hold
when stony ground
drilled holes in idiotic souls
believing lies told so long even right seems wrong
foolishness gripped and ripped away all common sense

running with scissors and rose colored glasses
hell has enlarged herself
the devil has fooled the masses
what a shame we didn't listen
to the preaching when it was convenient
but it's not too late to escape
a remnant will be saved

tricked by your own convictions
the rapture finally came
left empty silently praying
for God to shorten the days
remain brave
no quarter asked none is given
with Christ all can be forgiven
But before all that happens
looking back we ponder the power of unbelief
what a relief if you avoided the thief
stop listening to the devil the great pretender
it's not too late just don't stay deceived
in Christ you must believe
it's the reason He came to set your spirits free

When time reveals itself
and the truth becomes clear
hear the voice
that shows you your place and how to behave
evil came disguised in a masquerade
throwing shade
but being brave is more than standing still
its engaging your will in God's divine plan for your life
get it right
and stop listening to devil's lies he's just a great pretender

Silly Rabbit

Silly rabbit
Wake up!
Don't you know how valuable you are?
Dirty mouth and trashy dressing
Leaving chastity behind like it's a curse and not a blessing
Keeping your panties on and your mouth shut
Just made your stock go up
Let me upgrade you
And tell you what salvation is about
It's in the saving of your soul
Where you get real clout
You can shake your tambourine all you want in church
All that twerking and booty popping you just dropped like a
hot rock to the bottom of nothingness
Don't let the world get you twisted
Playing the harlot and looking like jezebel on crack
Don't make you all that
Will somebody please bring the spirit of Mary back
I want to look in the whites
Of your Alice in wonderland eyes
And tell you the truth
Purity will assuredly get you a king and a ring sing!
Stop settling
It's not about shaking your money maker
Trying to get you some paper
It's about living in God's favor
being blessed by the Savior
Come on silly rabbit
And make it a habit to live holy
Only you can prevent your soul from hell's fire
Holla!

amnesia

I knew I was suppose to remember something
that I didn't want to forget
but life got in the way and things started to get scary
distracting in everyway
shattering the tranquil ambiguity
until one day
a glimmer of something remembered
made its way into my private space
like a knock on the door of my mind
there was a rhyme a humming sound
the voice of a little girl singing a song
a melody that struck a nerve in time
and something illusive barely tangible
started and avalanche of something sweet and unique
like a peek into the mystical gardens of my youth
the safe place
and a tear ran down my face
a memory kept safe
driven deep into the recesses of my mind by all the chaos of
life and living
I hummed the song some more
waiting for the missing words to form
praying God help me shake depression
and a certain sadness that almost killed me
I carry those burdens no more
Casting my cares at my Savior's feet
I acknowledge my release for I've always been free
Amnesia is inconvenient
but the Holy Spirit knows how
to bring something back to your remembrance

so as the flood gates open
and I continue to hum
there's a rejoicing
knowing nothing past or present
has the ability to keep me from my purpose
so all those memories that laid dormant
can't hurt me
so I sing new songs
knowing I was called before I was born
and learn why amnesia served as a great escape
whether I allowed tolerated or permitted it
it's time to get on with living it
Life is what you put in it
and Amnesia
wasn't getting it done
so it's time to wake up
and take back control
know that God is always with you
if trust is your issue
realize God kept His promise when He gifted you
despite all your forgetfulness
of the little clues to your existence
God maintained His persistence
that Amnesia would not be permanent
but a secret weapon keeping precious
a song that is the joyful hum of our inheritance
our giftedness our talents magnify the testimony
what our life has truly become
So don't let amnesia be your excuse why you refuse to be
What God sent you here on earth to do
Wake up and remember
Let daily prayer be filled with answers

as the Holy Spirit brings things back to your remembrance
Do you know what you're here for?
I'm not letting not knowing
be a convenient excuse anymore
God is constantly talking
but are we really listening or just lazy and using forgetting
as a reason why we haven't prospered or gotten further along
in life
Try as I might
I still don't know why
God makes purpose such a mystery
some come to earth gifted
and immediately operating
and other's like me
spend years searching
until the past and life experiences presents its offering
I am born into being through life and living
and what I did not remember at birth upon entering the
earth
no longer hurts
Amnesia holds no power Forevermore

"…and that's the soulful thing about playing,
you offer something to somebody,
you don't know if they'll like it, but you offer it."
-Wynton Marsalis
To a Young Jazz Musician: Letters from the Road

Selah

When the music stops for a moment too long
and there's a ringing in your ears
the slap is the last thing you hear
something inside breaks
and is driving you
moving you
they tried to beat it out of you
scream it out of you
rip it from your very soul
but the music still carries on
so don't let it go
Selah
You are driven beyond all comprehension
I have never seen the righteous forsaken *Psalm 37:25*
the right doing right
living right
talking right walking right
The *righteous*
so is my sense of forlornness
all my struggles an indication
that I am forsaken
and not "righteous" enough to garner God's favor
Selah
Abused as a child I carry a death scar of a childhood robbed
strange thoughts take root
I've seen things and done worse to boot
Selah

Pausing to breathe
I believe

what I say
and I know that when I close my eyes
I see things differently
not as the world deceives me to believe
I walk this earth with my feet above the dirt
above the grave just barely
alive
just breathe
Selah
when the music stops
and the note is sustained
lingering
as the melody quietly fades
and the musician's wait
a rest in tempo
the pause vibrates its silence
emphasis is put on the statement
attesting to and agreeing with
we are forever changed
Selah
my life is such a pause
when the music stops
and God is trying to get your attention
a stillness happens in the atmosphere
an occurrence most are not aware
Still is the voice
a sudden break that appears seemingly without warning
just a knowing
all my Selah's were thought provoking
a spoken word
reflection evoking
I speak into the quiet when I know only God is listening

the deafening quiet of
Selah
I cherish those moments in time
when God is about to do a new thing in my life
I am apprehended
held in suspense by the possibilities
of the next crescendo
right before the music stops
I sense the switching of the tracks
a changing of the guards
when God tells me now is the time to do my part
when the world has had its say
and I've talked till I'm blue in the face
listening to God
puts Selah in place
listening to the still small voice directing your every way
each note a new song sung
a new day begun
Selah
when the music stops
and life hits you with a blow that shocks
the clock moves slow as time seems to stand still
and it takes every part of you to recuperate and regain your
will
no matter how long it takes to recover
it's never too late to discover
that Selah can just be a praise break to our Heavenly Father
even When the music stops
Selah is enough.

I turned on myself

To hide in myself
Almost destroying myself
Then I learned in a place all by myself
How to see and love myself
Everyday I talk to myself
Don't give up
Don't give in
Stay true to the vision
In the end you will win
It's been a real struggle just to survive
I was full to the breaking
Cracking at the seams
But I looked up to heaven
To make real my dreams
I cry in the dark starry night
I cry in the bright sunlight
Tears on my face
Always seem right
I turned on my self
To hide myself
Almost destroying myself
Then I learned in a place all by myself
How to see and love myself
Everyday I talk to myself
I'm never alone
Through Christ I am made strong
I've been wonderfully changed
This life living thing is for real
a life without Christ
Is a devil willed shame
So don't give up the fight

Whatever battle you're in
And know that once this things is done
We really do win
In the arms of God you'll find real help everlasting
Erasing childhood pains
Shaking loose chains and strongholds
That claim our destines
I know passing the test
Means I did my best
I'm no longer the same
I refuse to walk away
I'm keeping my head in the game
So don't give up and don't give in
I promise you
He promised me
In a place all by myself
How to see and love myself
And as long as God and I agree
With the dreams He's promised me
Then whether I'm by myself or with somebody else
I'll be fine
Because God promised me all by myself

"No matter how far gone you've gone
you can always turn around...
Turn around turn around turn around
and you may come full circle
and be new here again."
-Gil Scott Heron
I'm New Here

in too deep down to the bone

in too deep
down to the bone
I can't even sleep
I don't know why
I feel a tear on my face
I brush it away

the pain is intense
why can't say
all I know is everyday
I feel the same old way
grief and a certain defeat wrecks havoc
the heart deferred made sick
pain becomes a burden
I stand tough determined
to uproot this deep seated lie masquerading as the truth
this addictive behavior
is no mere illusion
praying for a miracle
some kind of solution
why this dark pain has found its integral intrusion
my soul screams
I'm trapped behind enemy lines
I try repeatedly to conquer the beast
beating walls with fists this dream is deceiving so why is my
heart bleeding
I look to The Cross
divine healing is what I'm most needing
in too deep and down to the bone
I can hear the lyrics to Gil Scott Heron's last song

"...turn around turn around and you may come full circle
but, be new here again..."
like staring at my face in the mirror
déjà vu becomes my proof
that God does hear you
because I've been here before and even then He brought me
through a certain sin
so I take solace
that hope carries
and faith sustains
I'll keep praying in Jesus name
In too deep to quit
down to the bone
this is it
every time I make another attempt
I'm different and as gifted
I'm lifted to another dimension by the experience
so this poem is written
surely I'm not the only one
battling some strange addiction

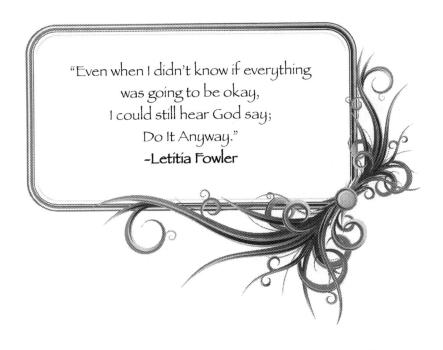

"Even when I didn't know if everything
was going to be okay,
I could still hear God say;
Do It Anyway."
-Letitia Fowler

ECHOES of a Promise

Fortified with a resolve to try harder
reach farther
refusing to barter my destiny
for a wallet full of currency
my very presence
the reason I am alive
and still breathing
I am the Echo of a Promise
it lingers in the atmosphere
telling me
my grandmother's life was not in vain
I am the seed that still remains
destined
here for a purpose
I see the sky
in its never ending vastness
and I feel lost and insignificant
but I grasp its endless possibilities
raising my hand to heaven in silence
I know God knows what I am thinking
why I'm the lucky one
the church folks say I'm blessed
Despite the cards I've been dealt
And the awful way I've felt at each death
Still my heart melts
With hopefulness
there is nothing else
For me to do nothing left for me to prove
I am the last and I am the first
Assuring that the Echoes of the Promise is fulfilled through me

Because of what my ancestry could not do
I exist
God caused my existence
My very presence provoked resistance
2 or 3 times I almost died
But God was insistent that I be alive
That my ancestors cries not be pushed aside
No test was ever invented that a child of God
could not survive
So I'm alive still
To fulfill
The Echoes of a Promise
Through boats and ropes
I am your hope
I am the echo of a promise
I hear your moans and cries lingering in my soul
In both pleasure and in pain
You've willed my legacy to bare no shame
because I breathe your name
Josephine Clementine (Nana) Estelle (Essie) Carolyn Betty
Duchess Arnold Norman Arthur Duke Marie Lula and James
It's because of you
There is a me
And I stand high on your shoulders
To proclaim
I will be brave
If I am the only one to speak out loud your names
Through me you'll be able to say because of God
I am the *Echo of a Promise*

Now that I'm awake

Now that I'm awake
I need to breathe fresh air
suffocated by all your convenient lies
falling from your deceitful eyes
a malaise
has crept into these irrelevant relationships
my faith in you
has been compromised
but I will not become self condemning
for the masquerade you've successfully delivered for so long
I declare finished
and deceives me no more
Now that I'm awake
I know how to fix these mistakes
I'm letting discernment have her perfect place
I'm letting God pick my friends from here on out
doing business with enemies has got to stop
and when it comes to family
Well, I'll love them at a distance

Now that I'm awake
I can take my place
in purpose on purpose
deliberately using faith
I'm not waiting for the final curtain
what I want God's got
It's obvious with Him my future is certain
Now that I'm awake
I'm taking a seat at the table
God has prepared for me
even in the presence of mine enemies Psalms 23:5

Now that I'm awake
I will be exactly what God has created me to be
I know I'm more than capable and no longer easily deceived
my life experiences have given me a certain wisdom
sensitivity to your intentions
not to mention
I've the Holy Spirit whispering
Now that I'm awake
I'm listening and attentive

You Know My Name

When first you meet me you call me your woman
my name is Eve
I hope you remembered what the Lord said
and you better make sure I know it too
stick close to me until I get it rote
cause if you don't then I won't
and we'll both be in a sinking boat
the first time you start acting up
like you're some Super fly King
and things start to look a little shaky
You know my name
just call me Esther
I'll be fasting three days to change this thing
we're all going to have to pray
if God is going to have His way
    Because a barren womb will not be satisfied
I cried
endless tears day and night
I finally struck a deal with the Lord
lend me a child just for a little while
You know my name
they call me Hannah
when others leave babies like unwanted parcels on door steps
I am the one most needing such a precious gift
and the Lord Blessed
the tears of Hannah garnered her request

when I laughed at the promise
I must have done it too loud
God called me on it but He made me a vow

through me will this miracle be even at ninety a baby is
conceived
You know my name it's the one God changed
Sara**i** when the "i" was me Sara**h** to know the "h" is Him

let's talk and sit by a tree
and discuss things from A to Z you can tell me anything
I love to listen no judgments here
like a prophetess with my African tresses
wisdom I impress it
years of living make me confess it
I am "a phenomenal woman" –Maya Angelou
You know my name
they call me Deborah
come let us sit under my palm tree
and I will tell you how we will get the victory

I am a seller of purple
a business woman who knows her worth and is not afraid to work
I contribute to the household
so what if I make double that's just less trouble for you to
worry about
it's my pleasure to make you look good
we'll have the best house even if it's in the hood
You know my name
They call me Lydia

Now, I stand before you as a testament
this promise from God gives me my confidence
cause when God gives you a name He doesn't make a mistake

So today I make sure my living is not in vain
You know my name
it's Letitia
and it means joy and happiness
my assurance comes from knowing all my blessings are met
with gratitude
and all my tests and trials only come to make me strong
so whether its in a poem or lyrics to a song
You'll know my name
I am your joy in the morning
Good morning.

This is what I know for sure
Baby Steps is walking
Psalms 37 gets you access
I'm talking heaven
So walk
And if you fall
Like Donnie sang;
"we fall down but we get up"
Seize the dream
Nothing is as it seems
Inherit the earth
Laughing
The devil is a defeated foe
If only you'll believe it as though obstacles only come to
make you strong
Wait without fear and receive bountiful blessings
Speaking the Name
Jesus
God is with us
This is what I know for sure
Any forward progress counts
Just never give up
What would be the point then
To stop before the victory begins
Take hold of the vision
And see God move mountains
Even on trembling feet
Baby steps is walking

I will bring you out

It's almost over
But it occurred to me
That
Before it started
I was already free
now that the time has come
For all the world to see
That when Jesus makes a promise
It's a fait accompli

When the heart is weak
And can barely beat
Validation as proof is a powerful weapon
Like a revelation Jeremiah 15 spoke to me
Can't you see the hand of God working
No matter where you end up
You're right where you're suppose to be
Your victory is guaranteed
No matter how long the trial
He whispers these words of comfort to my trying soul
I will bring you out

Tears of Hannah

Digging deep
I cried out to God
From the precipice from the abyss
I didn't ask for this
The ravages of life have mutilated my soul
Torn into shreds
I looked all around
wondering why I wasn't six feet under ground
Barrenness castrated my femininity
Salvation didn't stop life from happening
I agonized over its duplicity
I was thrown in the fire
Lost in the wilderness
I've seen death and despair
Does anybody out there care

Forced to my knees
I stare vacantly into the void
Seeing nothing blinded by pain
Trembling lips emits a sigh
Forcing me to realize
Only the power of God can keep me alive

I bow my head once held high
And surrender letting pride fall to ashes
Like heaven is watching I pray
Passionately and intense
With the Tears of Hannah on my breath these prayerful
words surface

Dear Lord God
My redeemer the very owner of my soul
In misery I see how manipulating life
Creates strife and dissension
You're putting me in an awkward position
I'm holding onto a promise that I now have to evaluate different
Further words fail me
I just need you to deliver me from the awful situation

Falling prostrate
I let the tears fall as I make sense of it all
I'm left paralyzed
Weeping but I'm eating
Living without being
Praying without speaking
My mind roams while I'm thinking
Can I appeal make a deal with God
Beseeching forever reaching
I seek the mercy seat
The chamber of the Divine
Crawling under the veil in my mind
Relief is what I find
As I look to God for defense
A sanctuary for my soul
Time has no place
Just breathe and release
The misinterpretation of the dream and wait
Knowing that with God there are no mistakes
Just surrender and permit
With His phenomenal power He equips
I went to God overwhelmed and crushed
But I left wiping the dusting of tears off my face

Saying under my breath I'm still going to trust Him
And repurpose the life I have left
Still feeling bereft
My soul knows it's cried the Tears of Hannah

and things

I told Him about my pain and things
He showed me my future and things
Opening up my soul and things
Told me how obedience brings
Victory and things
God said Come after Me and I'll give you all those things
Seek Him while He can be found
And He'll give you joy and peace and things
Don't let the devil keep turning you around
In Christ you have found a Savior
He walked across the water and things
Healed the blind and raised the dead and things
Died on the Cross and rose in three days and things
And you're worried about money and things
He's got streets paved with gold and things
Cattles on a thousand hills and things
Trust God and see what His salvation will bring
I'm talking about heaven glory peace and power and things
It's time we let go of the past and things
And start to embrace Jesus for the redemption He brings
He leads me through the valley and things
Over mountains and through valleys and things
I'm not afraid of no shadows of death and things
He's prepared a table before me and anointed my head and things
When I've got Jesus I've got all I need and things
Because He's faithful He's glorious and He's worthy and things
it's time for the choir of angels to sing
There's not enough words to express what He means to me
and things
He loved me until I loved Him back and things
Until I learned to worship Him right and things
when Christ gave me Himself He gave me everything.

Cool In The Dark Starry Night

I found my true calling
Listening to God calmed my tattered soul
I repositioned myself
Juxtaposition to the plan
It was only then that I could see things more clearly

When my attention did not compete with my destiny
I became focused and single-minded
Hope hit its mark
And sparked wanting of the possibilities
At the breaking of a new day God would wipe clean my slate
And wipe away all my past mistakes
No longer trying to dictate my course
without checking with God first
Every choice every chosen path
Should line up with God's Word
You do the math
You know when you're doing something wrong and results
are taking too long
'Lord thy Words have I hid in my heart
That I might not sin against thee' Ps 119:11

This is how I see it now
If I'm in the right place
What I need will come to me
That's the divine order of things
My structure is safe
My foundation in place
It was a cool dark starry night
When I realized I really was covered by God's grace
No longer traveling that long hard road of rationale
Detonating bombs in my soul with I told you so

All my choices led me to this place
Laying in a hospital bed with IVs in my arm
In this room death no longer hides in the shadows
And fear is a scare tactic
That finds its roots in my desperation
Screaming now seems fake and staged
and crying is for babies
Yet hot salty tears flow from my shattered eyes and fall off
my wobbling chin
Trying to comprehend what the doctor said again
Disbelief frames my face and nails it to the wall
Martyred for poetic justice
whose expression bleeds anguish
The shutter clicks
And the picture of all my life
Lays stuck trapped behind my grief-stricken eyes

Change is imminent
Decision is the breaking of the glass
Class is now in session
Now faith is real faith and your only defensive weapon
The narrow road I must follow
Full of falling rocks
I block with my helmet of salvation
Protecting my screaming soul
Choose!
Who will you serve
Who's words will you allow
To spew from your mouth
It's a matter of life or death
Your tongue has the power
To open a cave full of Ali Baba's gold or dig your own grave

I speak to my tattered soul
Still feeling how the earth shook beneath my feet
ignoring the death toll of the doctor's words
I reach deep up to my spiritual light
Illuminate my mouth Holy Spirit
I speak life
I shall live and not die
Whatever I have to try
Whatever I have to do
I will not be satisfied
Until restoration has found its rightful place at my side
Deep within my soul I knew
I will never forget the effects of that cool dark starry night.

Cracked Mirror

Shards of broken glass
Lay abandoned
being careful how I handle it
I peruse my distorted reflection
passing judgment upon inspection
I conclude I am not who you say I am
I fan away negativity
like a pesky fly
and instead search deep inside
until I find my true authentic self
Jesus was never recognized He was always revealed Bishop Jones
So how can I deny that my presentation to the world will be
misunderstood
misinterpreted and always subject to the wrong impression
I nevertheless take the challenge
to find balance
in a world often not fair
seemingly without a care
who gave the 2% the right to decide what I wear
looking in that cracked mirror
I learn to let go of all those preconceived notions misguided
dispositions
choosing rather to listen
to the cultivated voice of my instincts
where God speaks softly but is clearly heard through the
chaos and noise

His voice reinforces my strong resolve
to get the true image of me right
I have the authority

to see me as worthy
I am a child of God
Not from birth but from being born again
that was when
A new thing was being done
even a cracked mirror can't take from me
what man never gave me
selectivity is my prerogative
certain restrictions do apply
I want to live the sanctified life

Looking up to the Son
I am revived to claim the promise
Stepping into the light
I'm singing a new song
Cracked mirrors and broken glass
can not cast a bad reflection of me
it's up to me to see the me God created me to be

So I shake the dust from my feet
Stepping through the debris
of your distorted view of me
it does not nor can it ever define me
nor can it limit what I will eventually be

I've got angels whispering on my shoulders
You're an over comer
You are more than a conqueror
You are creatively and resourcefully made
You human being
You are free to achieve the impossible
Even being forgiven

so let nothing
especially not the distorted views of cracked mirrors
i.e., other people's dispositions
the look in their eyes is not your true reflection
I stand more convinced after listening
I am my own testimony
My life tells its own story
I live to give God the glory
Smashing that looking glass
I see myself more clearly
Stronger wiser indomitable
I am a winner
A sinner saved by grace
can't you see the victory written all over my brand new face

When at first light
the sun rose high
offering its protection
I caught hold of my reflection
in the cracked mirrors facsimile
blurring what God saw as perfection
sometimes its easier to breathe when you realize
how these lying eyes can't predict when God has pre-
orchestrated your life
doubt says what you see here on this plain is real and dreams
unseen are fake
Faith says look beyond the fake here and see the real there
unseen seen and made real
my intellect was challenged
by the cracked mirrors perspective
delusion yelled
Physician heal thyself

and erase the fake resemblance
Cracked mirrors yield
There is no truth in them
I'm trying to tell you
Cracked mirrors
are nothing but false images appearing as real
so stop listening to the devil

Soulful

quiet words whispered
from a victorious soul
told
of stories old
how fighting the flesh is never wrong
bested the battle royal
before doubt fell
hope springs eternal
like lively stones
Rejoice
I rose from the debris of scattered dreams those memories
quietly proclaiming soon
Victory
it's comfort God has given me
after pain as I live and breathe
maintaining a certain dignity
Humbly
I bow knowing
only God can judge me
my life experiences qualifies me
and using those experiences benefits the rest of us
I exist as a gift
Sacrificed just a little bit
I never knew
that my pain
had the impact
to change
someone else's life

So I testify
living my life openly in truth
showing you
that no matter what you go through
if you yield your heart to God
there is no sin
that can stop the completion of the task
God has assigned to you

So I pray
letting my soul still away to a safe place
in my now faith attitude
I let God's kingdom decide my altitude
quietly my soul sighs
as the platform of my ministry
takes shape in my mind
I let the perpetual motion of life
move me forward
toward the lessons I must learn
I use my words wisely finally
Learning how my open mouth debacles
led to great calamities

So I speak life
stepping through the door
with a prophetic voice
and soulful expressions that never grow old
like Lord let your will be done
and Father give us this day our daily bread
with a bowed head I take it on the chin

once singing life must be mean to me
now I'm saying all things are possible
if you only believe

So I'm taking this journey called life more seriously
experiencing all the glorious benefits
of being
Soulful

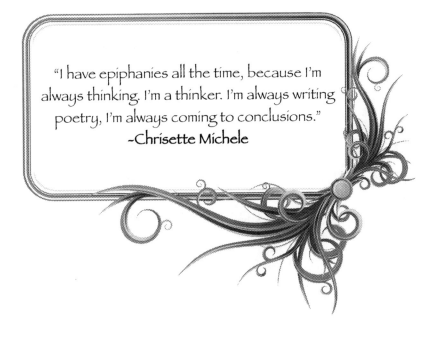

"I have epiphanies all the time, because I'm always thinking. I'm a thinker. I'm always writing poetry, I'm always coming to conclusions."
-Chrisette Michele

just like an epiphany

my mind thinks
and I become
my hearts beats
and I feel
everything wonderful in the world that's real
I am still
and I hear more clearly and peace follows me
impossible means nothing
my flesh is subject to my will
Spirit within help me conquer the beast
daily praying
constantly saying
I will live and not die
and it hit me
just like and epiphany
this world is tailored made for me
and I exist in it to fulfill my destiny
nothing created
no man made entity
can conqueror me
no devil brave
or evil intentions targeting me
will stop what God has declared is providence
what will be will be
my mind thinks it
I learn to speak it
and I become what I believe
and it hit me
just like an epiphany
why do I fear anything
freed from preconceived fallibility

just breathe
and let God enlighten me
tender is my heart
humbled before the Lord
if I can see God in me great and mighty
then pain and suffering
tell its own story
all that I endure gives God the glory
without mumbling or grumbling
letting the fruit of spirit have its perfect work
trials teach me
how real life can be
but then it hit me
just like an epiphany
serve the Lord and Him alone
and everything
will be as it's suppose to be
through the storms and the heavy rains
when the sun shines bright with its golden rays
the cool wind breeze on summer days
through stifling heat and more bills to pay
still I can say
no devil brave
nothing man made
can stop me
when God declares this life is prearranged
I will be brave
no matter how scary
from the cradle to the grave
I am a child of destiny
and it hit me
just like an epiphany
life with God is more than serendipity

Just a little more

Just a little more
is all it takes to get whatever it is you're after
So don't give up just yet
You're almost there
Just a little more

"I wasn't defined by my failures, but by the grace
in which I rose again"
-TD Jakes

It was a repositioning
a focus change
a new direction ordained
the game stayed the same
what was different was my name
and a fine tuned frequency
that came straight from heaven
several false starts seemingly
the Holy Spirit master route manipulator
exactly no coincidence no accidents
I respond to truth my proof is that I'm right beside you
know that I see you
and that something familiar about your spirit breathes quietly
don't let go
discernment was learned
a hard lesson that
but nothing can take away
the fact that God has my back
it was a repositioning
a focus change
a new direction ordained
a name change
even though the game stayed the same
what a shame
digging for treasures
when a man's soul is worth more than what you find in the dirt
anything you can carry in as wallet or a purse or lock in a safe
has little worth coming from the earth
we run around in circles drawing lines in the sand
over gold and oil and the perfect place to live
that's not the plan
how can man get it all so terribly wrong

It was a repositioning a rebirth
when I learned my worth
Far above rubies Proverbs 31:11
we come from the dirt
but it was the breath God breathed into my nostrils
that increased my worth
a soul and spirit that can not die
eternity is why
I felt a name change
like Sarai to Sarah
the miracles God performs
showed me importance to a certain degree
It was a repositioning
a focus change
that gave me an opportunity to live again
with pockets empty
I stand in silence
knowing that the intangible force of my worth was not
material
but intrinsic and gift centered
for all of my life
if I could but walk worthy of the calling
then all my trials will have their perfect end
It was a repositioning a focus change a new direction
ordained
that made me proclaim
God just changed my name

Blind Ambiguity

Living with impunity
straddling fences
being lukewarm is a nuisance
and inundated with consequences

Getting away with talking
and saying nothing
I'm calling for conviction
confidence of silence and certainty
without wishy-washy dispositions

I don't have time for all the vagueness
and hazy commentary
It's just foolish prattle

Our life's struggle is to find centeredness
focusing on God and His Son
is our resolute mission

Yet I'm left sifting through
all the fragmented and vague
empty sentences
conversations that leave
something valuable missing

I've found my journey hindered
by all that empty rhetoric
If you've got the mike
and you're standing in the limelight
then please

can you use your anointing
and say something that might
be filled with meaning
and significance to me

Or just shut up speaking
in riddles that are empty
pounding your chest
is an easy distraction
what a hot mess
obstructing without meaning
It's just blind ambiguity

The machinations of the mind
are hard to define
your random speechifying
should be your life long crime
It's diabolical
bordering on demonic
wasting our time
trying to interpret
your idioms and lies
again and again
it's just empty rhetoric I find

But when the anointed
has the publics interest
at the forefront of their rhymes
It's reason we find
that fills our imaginative young minds

Even through my own poetic revealing
I have discovered and found my own healing

it was the thought
that ambiguity is a lesson that costs
us our future that's lost
Is anybody looking to the Cross

But I am encouraged nonetheless
To keep up the good fight
for we wrestle not
against flesh and blood
let's come in love
the idea is to be harmless as a dove
dealing with each other in kid gloves
Instead of with all the fluff and empty stuff
Erase your mendaciousness
to leave God and His Son out
of our anomalous debates
don't be fake
let's set aside all our clever ingenuity
it's nothing anyway but
Blind Ambiguity

**STOP
BEING
SO AMBIGIUOS
ABOUT
EVERYTHING!**

'higher power" "the universe" "energy"
is packed with ambiguity
most will at least acknowledge
GOD
but only the truly committed
to life eternal
will say
JESUS IS LORD

"An artist must be free to choose what he does, certainly,
but he must also never be afraid to do what he might choose."
-Langston Hughes

Quit believing the lies

Quit believing the lies
and stop acting like
everything God ever promised you
doesn't mean a thing

we walk this earth
deceiving ourselves
as if the breath we're breathing
is supplied by the ambiguous "universe"
you curse yourself spouting untruths
creating an atmosphere
that in ignorance you choose
deciding what you'd rather do
instead of listening to God
compromising half your life
is witchcraft
insidious and sneaky
it creeps upon you
weighing your odds
contemplation
leads to the easy way out
shrugging you say "whatever"
realize "obedience is better than sacrifice" I Samuel 15:22
remember this is your *one* life
reincarnation is a fake escape
and the bigger mistake is thinking hell isn't real
don't let all the little lies of compromise
lead you to thinking you've found the easy way out

Quit believing the lies
the conscious mind knows always

what the spirit says to the prophet
listen carefully
it's not worth the sacrifice to believe
the lie
you only deceive yourself
creating a certain future calamity
believe me when I say
I've been there before
the lies we tell ourselves
based on some half truth we heard but never proved
but God is about to purge what you misunderstood
if you just pray and seek God's face II Chronicles 7:14
you'll stop wasting valuable time you no longer have

no matter what the price
get your mind back on track with God's word
The kingdom of heaven suffered violence Matthew 11:12
know that giving your best effort
and taking the best offered from God
is your truth
and an integral part of your character
the devil is a liar
So Quit believing the lies
and find why
every time you get close to victory
things go awry
it's a lie
but to the untrained eye
you think seeing smoke means fire
and all that calamity that befell Joseph and he did nothing
things are not always as they seem
dreams do come true
if you Quit Believing The Lies

"You've got to go get it, go do it, and do it right."
-Doc Rivers

The Last Word

I had to almost die
to realize
time was not necessarily on my side
its passing leaves me dissatisfied
trying to put mistakes behind me
I find life an amalgamation of catastrophes
so I write to you from a place of respect
Knowing the decisions I made and suffer the cost of time lost
can be reversed
With God all things are possible
see me and know
it's all really redeemable

I walk this earth
having had tasted and touched way too much
sins egregious to my soul
I know temptations are still waiting
these fleshly appetites are never satisfied
so I write
in hopes that one day
all my wounds would have healed
But until then I'm walking by faith
I'm doing it God's way
writing dreaming and believing
Waking up Alice will be my first seed offering
Alice's Adventures in Wonderland is a fantasy created by
Lewis Carroll
and in that story she too was dreaming
but the saddest commentary
is that some of us refuse to wake up

and be about the vision God imparted to us
age 48 slapped me hard in face
I wound up in emergency close to dying
of congestive heart failure twice
imagine having to think to breathe
you can't even sleep
your heart hurts struggling to beat
and prayer's don't come easily
when you can hardly breathe
I just needed God to hear me silently
even through my wheezing and receive
my silent screams
of a dreams about to die
more than a conqueror Romans 8:37
made me realize
I was never really in danger of dying
as long as these gifts buried deep inside
hadn't seen the light of day
There's no way I'm leaving this earth but empty

So I rise from my sick bed and write
these words are mine
instinct tells me really by the Holy Spirit
no matter how insignificant irrelevant redundant or repetitive
these words compose my life in poetry

Now at 52 I declare
this is only the beginning
as I go walking the earth I'm learning
as long as I'm breathing
I will not stop until empty
It's not about a degree or even about money

it's about living my Zoë my God kind of life
as a servant of my Lord and Savior Jesus Christ
I try everyday to get this living thing right
and being alive is all I need to be to be qualified
it's never too late to dig up your gift
and tell the world why you're here
God created you for a purpose
and now is the time to be about it

Waking up Alice

stop procrastinating and let your gifts see the light of day
and know that today is a good day
it's never too late